The Busyness of Starting a Business:

A Practical Guide to Starting a Business

By Ronald E. Watkins

TLM Language Services Co., LLC

Atlanta

TLM Language Services Co., LLC
1100 Peachtree St. NE
Ste. 200
Atlanta, GA 30309
www.tlmlanguageservices.com

Ordering Information:
For details, contact busybusinessbooks@gmail.com or Amazon.

Print ISBN: 978-1-952192-00-5

First Edition

TLM Language Services Co., LLC
Atlanta

Table of Contents

Acknowledgments

I want to acknowledge those various entities that gave me the opportunity to gain experience and enhance my business knowledge. Although I have experienced several ventures that many people would view as failure, I have found that a business venture is only a failure if the entities involved in the enterprise do not learn from these experiences. Every successful individual throughout history has had setbacks or not achieved his or her initial goals, but the failures eventually lead to success.

I also want to acknowledge individuals whose stories motivated me to strive, overcome obstacles, and reach for success: specifically, my maternal Grandmother, Flossie H. Valentine, DPM; her brother Horace Hague, DDS; and my mother, Joan M. Valentine, DPM. These individuals persevered in their professions, despite barriers of race and gender.

Additionally, I wish to acknowledge my biological family: my wife, Yvonne; and our children, Russell, Kristina, and Kortney, for their support of many various business endeavors and for their striving in becoming good productive citizens for themselves, their friends and families, and their respective communities.

Furthermore, I want to acknowledge both my biological and surrogate family members and friends whose interactions add to my life experiences. You know who you are.

Lastly, I wish to acknowledge individuals and organizations that make it possible for those who wish to pursue their business dreams to have opportunities and assistance to do so. I discuss many of you in this publication.

Foreword

The *Busyness* of Starting a Business

What is this book about, and why was it written?

Someone once said that a book conveys a transfer of knowledge. After more than sixty years of being involved in business as an employee, business owner, accountant, and volunteer with both Junior Achievement and SCORE, I feel that my experiences will benefit those who are contemplating starting a business.

I have titled this book *The Busyness of Starting a Business.* In my experience, many people have expressed a desire to own or operate a business, but they never get started. Any worthwhile endeavor takes action and thus getting busy (i.e., as a bee).

I have given a lot of thought to the sophistication and tone of this writing. Since I identify my primary audience as people who do not have business degrees or have extensive experience in managing or running a business, I intend to present information in a less complicated and more understandable way. You are always free to use other reference materials to obtain additional data that may present other information not included here. The information presented here is based on my personal experiences and research into the stated history and/or purpose of cited specific organizations. Some other authorities may have a different interpretation or emphasis; likewise, you may disagree with the information presented, and you are welcome to present your point of view.

Another major issue for me in writing this book was deciding how technical it should be regarding language, concepts, and the multitude of tasks and other considerations people need to start a business. My experiences with counseling and teaching seminars about starting a business have led me to believe that the majority of people I have been in contact with have little formal business training and education, for example college degrees in business or associated disciplines. Additionally, I have found that people are more receptive if I use common language and examples.

Although I am not promoting any other business books or organizations, I have found a particularly reliable publication titled *The Small Business Start-Up Kit*. This publication, written by Peri H. Pakroo, Esquire, and issued by the NOLO Law for All Series, discusses many of the administrative and legal considerations of starting a business. Since this publication offers detailed coverage regarding starting a business, I will not attempt to duplicate this information per se, but to approach information that I wish to present in a manner that those in my primary audience have indicated is useful.

A lot of people decide that they want to go into business for themselves. Their reasons vary from self-actualization, a need to earn money after being laid off or fired, and a desire to make more money to the prospect of reaping better rewards for doing work similar to what they are already doing and wanting to be their own boss. This book is being written as a guide to:

- Making a decision to start or buy a business,
- Knowing what factors to consider in making this decision, and
- Following a method to achieve this goal.

I view the forming of a business and its maturation as having different stages:

1) Conception and Planning

2) Initiation and Start-Up

3) Consolidation of efforts to reach profitability

4) Expansion

The purpose of this particular book is to cover only the first two areas. I will discuss the other subjects in a later publication.

Many people desire to own a business. If you were to ask a dozen people to give their definition of a business enterprise, you would likely receive a dozen different answers. Most people make statements alluding to their vision of an operation and remark about some sort of business plan, usually from some template on a website. Some people who are seeking to establish a business are aware of administrative activities, such as obtaining a Federal Employer Number (EIN) or becoming a Limited Liability Company (LLC). Although these are useful elements in forming a business, these steps mark only the tip of the proverbial iceberg.

A for-profit business enterprise is an organization formed to provide a good (product) or service to a customer who is willing to pay a price for these items that are sufficient to cover the cost of providing them plus a reasonable profit to the business. Although most business enterprises are thought of as "legal entities" that can be done openly, there are other types of businesses such as criminal activity, unreported sales, or other work. Obviously, this writing concentrates on legal and legitimate businesses, which can be openly operated and have the potential to become profitable and socially acceptable.

Many people that I have assisted in planning or starting a business do not have business degrees from a college, or may have never worked in a position that develops skills that give them knowledge of various aspects of running a business. A major component of running and growing a business involves developing so-called people skills, which are essential in working with employees, contractors, vendors, customers, and other entities that affect the business. Also, aside from being an expert in the operational aspects of their business, the entrepreneur must be aware of the administrative requirements.

Since circumstances involving businesses constantly change, entrepreneurs must continually update their knowledge. They can accomplish this feat through attending seminars, seeking formal business education, reading relevant information, interacting with associations and organizations involved in the industries that affect their business, and networking with others who can offer insights into improving a business.

In Conclusion

For me, what is yet to come is connected to the past. Societies change over time. People in any society are linked to what is familiar to them as well as the new changes that are coming. Entrepreneurs need to understand the connections between past events and circumstances and what they can portend for future opportunities.

Special Addendum

Although the information in this book was completed before the Worldwide Coronavirus Pandemic was announced in February-March 2020, the basic principles regarding starting a business remain relevant; however, businesses' activities are part and partial to societal needs and dependent on the marketplace. I feel that it is important to place the actions involving a start of a business in context with the reality of the current business environment.

Everyone is aware that the mandated shutting down of certain types of businesses has had a tremendous impact on who can still operate, what changes an existing business can make to retain some level of business activity, and who will survive the crisis and return to being a viable business. Many of the programs initiated by government entities, nonprofit organizations, and direct donation programs have emphasized retaining employees or giving business capital to pay bills in order to remain in business. Since this crisis is still ongoing as of this writing, the final outcome is far from certain. This leads to questions regarding the wisdom of contemplating starting or staying in a business. Judging by numerous conversations over the past several months that I have had with persons who are currently in business and also those considering business, I find that there is still a great interest in starting or sustaining an enterprise, even in the face of the current environment. I wish to point out several considerations that someone in the above-cited positions should consider.

If one goes back in the histories of the United States and the world, there have been numerous periods where events such as war and pestilence have disrupted societies and economies. Many events have led to severe consequences for people, such as death, mental and physical suffering, and economic disruption. The fact remains that humans and civilizations are still here, and things are getting better. Events such as the current pandemic have led to great advancements in science and disease prevention. Economic conditions for the most part will improve, and there will be new opportunities for individuals to progress.

Unfortunately, many small and even some large businesses will cease to exist; however, it is evident that many businesses were at risk due to changes in technology (internet shopping), customer taste and preferences (the demise of malls and the consolidation of entities in various business segments), and also the normal churn of business coming into and leaving the marketplace. These kinds of situations existed prior to the event and will always be part of economic activity.

As I have indicated within this book, there are four primary stages in a business's cycle:

1) **Prebusiness planning**, which takes into consideration factors that will allow an enterprise to start

2) **Start-up**, which involves the commencement of business activity, including meeting operational and administrative requirements

3) **Consolidation**, when a business is operating at a level where they pass the break-even point, and future activity seems assured

4) **Growth and expansion**, when the business continues profitability and meets changing situations

For businesses that have not started, the current environment is an opportunity to evaluate what can be done in the near future and other changes in their business plan that are more relevant to the current situation.

For current enterprises, decisions have to be made which determine if some adaptation of the operation or other uses for their resources can be made to sustain some level of business activity.

For current businesses which cannot adapt as an enterprise due to the current situation, a decision has to be made to suspend or close the business.

Hopefully, we will survey this crisis, and societies and people will get through this.

My Story

Who Am I and Why Should You Care?

A lot of people claim to be experts at something. A person's expertise is usually associated with titles, degrees, certifications, and experience. My business-related experiences as well as formal education and training are detailed in this section. I also believe that my propensity for observation and analysis have assisted me in reaching many of the ideas presented in this work. You, the reader, can determine if my statements have any validity and are useful.

Who Were My Primary Influencers and Motivators?

My major influencers in having a strong desire to go into business were my maternal grandmother, Dr. Flossie Hague Valentine; her brother, Dr. Horace Hague; and my mother, Dr. Joan Marie Valentine. Part of my admiration for these individuals stemmed from how they achieved their positions and how their businesses affected me and the larger group of my family members.

My grandmother, Flossie Hague Valentine, was born in 1894 in Dayton, Ohio. She was the oldest of three children, and her mother died when she was six years old. Although her father was still alive, Grandmother Valentine was raised mostly by her maternal grandmother,

Mary Hinton, who was a freed slave. In the early twentieth century, most young African American girls were not expected to receive much formal education and more than likely would become domestic workers.[1] Grandmother Valentine completed two years of college. During that period, two years of college would have qualified her to become a teacher; however, she was not offered a teaching position. Since Dayton, Ohio, is in a northern state, there were no segregated schools where African American teachers would have been readily hired; therefore, the only position available to her was at the public library.

As Grandmother Valentine aged into her middle twenties, her grandmother, Mary Hinton, felt that she would end up being old and unmarried. Since Grandmother Hinton herself was becoming older and frailer, she suggested that Flossie marry a widower named John Valentine, who was twenty-one years older than Flossie. They had three children while in Dayton and two additional sons after moving to Chicago.

Grandfather Valentine had been a professional photographer, but due to some of his business failings, poor customer service, and the onset of the Great Depression—as well as his advanced age—he closed this business and did not seek other work.

After Grandfather Valentine closed his business, Flossie—at the urging of her brother Horace—moved to Chicago, where she entered a new medical specialty at that time known as *chiropody*, later renamed *podiatry*.

After receiving her license, Grandmother Valentine set up her chiropody practice in a small room at the front of a second-floor apartment on West Madison Street in Chicago. The front living room and

---

1   Explaining this dynamic in her essay entitled, "The Decline of Domestic Help," author Ester Bloom notes, "After the Great Migration brought multitudes of African Americans from the rural south to the urban north in the early twentieth century, black women took over the bulk of these [domestic] jobs. See https://www.theatlantic.com/business/archive/2015/09/decline-domestic-help-ma-id/406798/.

the outside of the apartment restroom were part of her business spaces. Her children, as well as other family members, resided in the adjoining rooms. She continued to pay rent and run her podiatry practice at this location for more than thirty years.

As the third oldest of her grandchildren, I spent a great amount of time with Grandmother Valentine and physically lived with her at the age of eleven, while in the sixth grade. That year, my grandfather and I were responsible for cleaning Grandmother's office and other spaces available for patients in the waiting room (the family front living room).

On February 22, 1952, I remember being out of school for George Washington's birthday. My grandmother asked me to go to a local grocery store. Although there was a larger store about a block away and around a corner, I elected to go across Madison Street. Madison Street is the main east/west street in Chicago, and at that time there were huge trolleys that ran on tracks on that street. In any case, after leaving the store, the next thing I remember was people standing over me as I went in and out of consciousness. I had collided with a streetcar. My physical damage was a broken pelvis, but I lived. What makes this episode so memorable is not almost getting killed at age seven, but that Grandmother Valentine told me that God kept me alive for a reason and that I would have to do, in her words, "great things."

My mother, Joan Marie Valentine Watkins Adams, was a bright student at Lucy Flower High School in Chicago. During this time, the local high schools were all-female or male-attended. Since she was such a good student—and since her mother was a practicing chiropodist— she was admitted to the Illinois College of Chiropody. Mom graduated from chiropody college while pregnant with me, and later, after remarrying, she had two additional children in 1949 and 1950.

While I was in the hospital following what I now fondly call the "streetcar accident," mom told me that she was buying a podiatry practice in Winnetka, Illinois, which is one of the most affluent suburbs on Chicago's North Shore. Because this suburb was some thirty miles from our home on the west side of Chicago, she would have to use a commuter railroad train to get to her office, and she would be away from home for approximately twelve hours each day. Mom felt it would give her an opportunity to advance in her profession and have a more lucrative business. My stepfather worked a 4:00 p.m.-to-midnight shift at the main US Post Office; therefore, my older brother, age ten, and I, age seven, became what are commonly known as "latchkey kids," meaning my parents expected my older brother and me to take care of ourselves. My stepfather's relatives, who lived in our apartment building at the time, took care of my younger brother and sister.

Grandmother Valentine called her brother, Horace Hague, a legendary "Renaissance man." He had a newspaper route as a young boy in Dayton, Ohio, and according to Grandmother Valentine, the Wright Brothers, who invented the airplane, were his clients. Grandmother Valentine told me that in his later teenage years he moved to Cincinnati, Ohio, and worked in a restaurant. After realizing that this was not the life that he wanted, he eventually moved to Boston, Massachusetts, where he attended dental college. He was also a concert-level violinist. He left Boston, and instead of returning to Dayton, he moved his family to Chicago, where he set up a dental practice.

When Great Uncle Horace learned that Grandfather Valentine had closed his business and that Grandmother Valentine's family situation was becoming precarious, he informed her that this new profession of chiropody was starting and that she could complete the curriculum within two years. He invited her—with her then three children and a retired husband—to move to Chicago, live with his family, and go to school.

Great Uncle Horace died in 1944, shortly after I was born. Although I never got to know or interact with him, tales about him as told by my grandmother became a major source of my inspiration.

Based on the medical legacy of my grandmother, great uncle, and mother, I stated at age ten that I would go into medicine. Throughout high school and college, I pursued a premedical curriculum. Eventually, I was admitted to Northwestern Medical School in Chicago in a physical therapy program, where I studied for two quarters of the four-quarter program. I withdrew due to other circumstances.

One of the greatest lessons that I have learned as I've gone through life is that things do not always go as planned, but you have to make the best of circumstances that come your way.

Why Is This Significant?

Motivation by mentors and events can inspire an individual's ambitions.

My Background and Experiences

In looking back on experiences that relate to my views and knowledge regarding "enterprise," I can categorize them into the following areas:

- Short-term job experiences,
- Other job experiences,
- Ideas and hustles,
- Businesses,
- Hobbies and interests,

- Organizations, and

- Education and training.

My Short-Term Work Experiences

As a teenager, I held an unpaid job as a farm hand at a farming-related summer camp. For a self-described "city boy," I enjoyed interacting with farm animals and crops.

As a result of having a positive attitude toward doing the farm work, the camp manager brought me back for another two-week period as a handyman. This job offered minimal pay for the work I completed. The following summer, the same camp hired me to work as the dishwasher and assistant to the camp's cook. This, too, was a paid position.

While in college, I worked several short-term jobs during the summer breaks. Some of these jobs were as a general laborer at the Procter & Gamble soap manufacturing plant in Chicago, various positions in small factories, and even as a short-order cook. Also, during my college tenure, I worked for two years as a dormitory assistant at my residence hall and held the position of campus movie projectionist. (Because racial segregation was practiced in this town, students at this HBCU had access to current movies through this program.) As a young adult, aside from business ventures and working other full-time jobs, I sold and cashed pari-mutuel tickets at the West Memphis Arkansas dog track for three years.

Why Is This Significant?

Even short-term jobs expose us to work and possible business opportunities.

My Jobs and Employment

While living in Chicago, I worked as a bacteria control technician for Central Soya Company for three months prior to starting classes at Northwestern University in physical therapy. Later, I worked as an elementary and middle school science teacher for two years (the infamous Cooley High). I also worked simultaneously as a driver for the US Postal Service for two and a half years in Evanston, Illinois.

In Memphis, Tennessee, I worked for two and a half years as a middle and high school math teacher (also volunteering as an assistant football and track coach). Keep in mind that traditionally, teachers did not get paid during the summer—and due to the fact that I lost my car because of business failures—I strategically obtained a position as a new car salesman for ten months at Buick, and then later for four years at a Chevrolet dealership. I also worked as a taxpayer service representative for the US Internal Revenue Service for a year and as an H&R Block income tax service representative for two seasons. For eight years, I worked as an investigator and mediator for the US Equal Employment Opportunity Commission (EEOC), and later was hired as a corporate-level senior EEO specialist for the Federal Express Corporation (FedEx).

In 1990, I moved to Atlanta, Georgia, to work as a senior personnel representative (local human resources manager) for FedEx, and retired in May, 2001.

Why Is This Significant?

These various positions led to first-hand experience in multiple aspects of business, including taxes, regulation, and the structure and workings of a large international corporation; they also demonstrate resiliency.

Self-Owned-and-Operated Businesses

Holiday Magic Distributor–Memphis, TN

I ran a multi-level marketing company for two years. Although this company did have excellent cosmetics and home-care products, their main emphasis was on recruiting other would-be entrepreneurs to build sales organizations and buy this company's products in massive quantities. I originally joined this company while still in Chicago, and I instituted their program after moving to Memphis. I became very involved in setting up the council of distributors in Memphis and eventually moved to the highest distributor level. Although I gave maximum effort to make this business a success, I changed the focus from recruiting others to become Distributors to building my own retail network. Eventually my business—and later the National Company—failed. In this new operation, my strategy involved using hair salons for retail sales, and using the home care products for fund raising with churches and schools.

R. E. Watkins Tax and Accounting Service

Having been trained and employed by the Internal Revenue Service, I used this knowledge to move into the taxpayer preparation business. After transferring from the IRS to another federal agency there was no longer a conflict of interest, and I was free to process tax returns privately. Not fully understanding how to charge for this work and other aspects of commercial income tax preparation, I worked for the H&R Block income tax preparation company for two seasons. Eventually, I gained numerous clients and established my own business and have continued to do so for more than forty year. In addition to the tax preparation work, I performed other accounting-related services for my growing business clientele.

Real Estate, Rental Properties, and Housing Rehab

Since I have always enjoyed building and renovations, I bought several blighted properties with the prospect of making them livable. Unfortunately, the current renters were unable or unwilling to pay a high enough rent to allow for the repairs that the county mandated, and that I, as the new owner of these properties had to perform. Eventually, I forfeited the properties to the county for back taxes.

During this time, I obtained a Real Estate license as an Associated Broker. In less than a year after entering this profession, home interest rates increased to more than 12%, which virtually shut down the market.

Having some carpentry skills, and willing to make some investments, I entered a joint venture with some other individuals in renovating and reselling distressed properties.

Norge Village Laundromat and Dry-Cleaning Service

After leaving the Memphis Office of the EEOC due to a reduction in force at that office, I elected to buy a laundromat business, which I ran with employees for more than seven years in two different locations. The primary operation was allowing the public to use my machines for washing and drying their clothing and other washable fabrics. During the first four years of the business, I managed employees who performed wash, dry, and- fold services. Additionally, we acted as a Dry Cleaning drop off spot (the actual work was performed by another vendor with whom we split the charges). On another occasion, I made my facility available to a nursing home who had to renovate its laundry room.

After seven years, I closed the business because of transferring with my full-time job to Atlanta.

Stairs by Designe

After retiring from FedEx (sixteen years with the company), I elected to open a specialized construction company. Our specialty was the sales and installation of spiral staircase kits. This decision was predicated on research into various factors such as capital requirements, competition, and a perceived need in the marketplace. While looking in a magazine, I noticed a company that manufactured a spiral staircase kit. I realized that in this market there were several homes that were being built with decks that did not have outside staircase access. After meeting with that company's management, a deal was made whereas I would buy their product at a wholesale price and could sale them at the advertised retail price. Additionally, my company could provide the installation. Over time we installed these items in lofts, apartments, and other locations where there is a limited space for a staircase. Additionally, over time we became a subcontractor to a local Staircase Manufacturing Company, which allowed us to bid jobs on high end homes where custom staircases were desired. Another primary operation involved the repairing, replacing, and renovation of various staircase components.

The US recession, which started in 2008, had a dramatic effect on various industries in the US and especially in building and construction. My business was severely affected, as were others in these industries. Because of this occurrence, I did not renew the lease for my outside office, and I laid off my regular employees. Although these circumstances impacted most of my business, I still managed to get some jobs. In 2015, due to my advanced aging and the physical toll that this work required, I officially closed this business.

Why Are These Businesses Significant?

As a former business owner, experiences in planning, operating, and interfacing with vendors, employees, and administrative entities are the basis for understanding how businesses function.

My Notable Hustles

Age 7

Sold Christmas cards after seeing an ad on the back of a comic book.

Age 21

Chartered a Trailways Bus to take fellow students from Kentucky State College to Chicago during the Christmas break. The first attempt failed due to many of the participating students backing out, and my deposit to the Bus Company was forfeited. The next year it was successful. This activity was important to those of us from the Gary, Indiana, and Chicago, Illinois, areas since it helped many of us avoid problems that we normally experienced when we had to transfer Greyhound buses in Louisville, Kentucky, due to competition for seats from soldiers from the nearby Fort Knox Army base, who were also traveling during the holiday season.

Age 25

Organizing a "home product"-based fund raiser with one of the largest Black churches in Memphis, Tennessee.

Age 31

Organized a fundraising program at a Memphis public school where students sold zodiac sign jewelry instead of candy and other traditional items used for this purpose.

Age 38

Bought, repaired, and managed twelve low-income rental properties in Memphis.

Age 41

Various home renovation and resell projects in Memphis.

Why is this significant?

Businesses require innovation and taking risks on new ideas.

My Hobbies and Interests

- Family activities

- Multiple sports fan

- Sports activity:

  - I entered college on a football scholarship. Later activities include being in organized softball, basketball, and tennis leagues. Currently, I am involved in health and fitness activities in my home gym and at health clubs

- Various carpentry projects:

  - Making cabinets and other construction projects

- Travel:

  - Trips to many American cities and other parts of the world

Why Is This Significant?

Although doing business and making money may be a passion, it is better to have a well-rounded life. Also, many businesses have started as a result of a hobby or other interest.

My Affiliations

- Kappa Alpha Psi fraternity (National Life Member)
- Prince Hall Masonic Lodge (Memphis, TN)
- Order of the Mystic Shrine (Shriner) (Memphis, TN)
- Former President EEO Council (Memphis, TN)
- Toastmasters International (Memphis, TN)
- Junior Achievement (Memphis, TN)
- Union Steward (AFGE 3599/EEOC-related government union, Memphis, TN)
- Student member of the Home Builder's Association (Atlanta, GA)
- Student member of the Southern Building Code Congress International (Atlanta, GA)

Professional Certifications

- The Institute for Applied Management and Law (Certificate in Employee Relations Law);
- Personnel Accreditation Institute (SPHR certification)
- Society for Human Resource Management
- Tennessee Board of Cosmetology (Licensed for three years in Memphis, TN)
- Tennessee Board of Real Estate (licensed as an associate broker for two years in Memphis, TN)
- SCORE certified mentor (Atlanta, GA).

Why Is This Significant?

Professional credentials and organizations are intricately involved in gaining experience, networking, and increasing useful knowledge.

My Educational and Professional Training

- Bachelor of Science degree from Kentucky State University with a major in biology and minor in chemistrySixteen semester hours completed toward teacher certification in the Department of Education at Northeastern Illinois University

- Twelve semester hours toward completing teacher certification in the Department of Mathematics at the University of Memphis, allowing me to teach math within the Memphis City Schools system

- 1,500 hours of training from the Corine College of Cosmetology, which allowed me to earn a license as a cosmetologist

- Independent study to take the Real Estate Examination given by the Tennessee Real Estate Board

- Earned twenty-four semester hours in accounting from the University of Memphis, which made me eligible to take the CPA examination

- Accumulated ninety quarter hours in Carpentry and Construction Management at Gwinnett Technical College.

Why Is This Significant?

Formal education and training are an integral part of gaining knowledge and skills.

Part I

Business Structures

Venues Used for Business

Forming or Starting a Business

Entrepreneurial Characteristics & Skills

Chapter 1
Business Structures

T he United States has various agencies and organizations that regulate business activities. The Internal Revenue Service (IRS) is the primary entity that sets the rules for business structure and reporting. They require an annual report (business tax return information) of businesses on specific forms. The type of return depends on the classification of the business (such as sole proprietorship or corporation). Although there may be some variation in business activities and missions, the following categories listed for profit-driven businesses are the only ones that may be used for the annual tax return. These reports are due by specific dates with specific information requirements. In addition to IRS-mandated tax returns, various state government entities may also have filing requirements.

States also play a role in formulating business structures. Corporations are formed at the state level by applying to the Secretary of State's office of the state having jurisdiction over the business. Although not a recognized filing business structure by the IRS, a form of business known as a *limited liability company* (LLC) is also formed at the state level.

Other government entities can control and regulate the activities of a business through licenses, permits, certifications, and other systems that give permission to conduct business activity within a particular jurisdiction. The judicial system at various levels can affect business activity through its interpretations of laws.

If you are playing a sport (or any game), you have to know the rules. In this section, I will discuss definitions of *business enterprises, small business, legal entity,* and *involved organizations.* For the sake of brevity, I am presenting the following information in basic terms. More detailed and current changes can be obtained from various relevant sources.

These are the primary recognized business structures:

*Non-Profit Businesses

Sections 501 C-3 and 501 C-4 of the IRS code allow businesses whose primary focus is social or political welfare to be treated differently from standard profit-driven corporations, in as much as these groups do not pay taxes on donations, grants, or proceeds received as part of their operations. These entities are required to use their proceeds, after expenses, toward their stated purpose. Individuals and other entities are also able to gain a tax deduction by donating to an approved organization. There are strict reporting requirements, and those who work for or manage these entities are considered employees and not owners.

Benefit and LC3 Companies

These are relatively new forms of business structures. A benefit corporation is legally required to prioritize a positive social impact in addition to making a profit for its shareholders. A low-profit limited liability company (LC3) is similar to a nonprofit company in as much as its primary purpose is to benefit the public; however, it is run like a for-profit business, with profits being a secondary goal. This type of business structure was formed so that charity-oriented LLCs could receive funds from large nonprofit foundations, per IRS rules that allow foundations to invest in businesses principally formed to advance charitable purposes. Currently, many states have adopted some form of this business structure. You should contact the Secretary of State in your respective jurisdiction to determine if a benefit corporation model exists.

*Sole Proprietorship

This is an individual who owns a business enterprise and is personally responsible for the profits, losses, and liabilities of the business operation. The owner reports the results of the business activity on a 1040 Schedule C form, which the owner files with his or her personal federal income tax return. This document is normally due on April 15 of the following year, if the taxpayer's business runs on a January-December fiscal year. The owner is also subject to self-employment tax on business profits.

*Partnership

Two or more entities—(they can be individuals or other partnerships)—form an enterprise in which these entities jointly operate the business. Profits and losses are shared as stipulated by the partnership agreement. The relative profits and losses are passed on to the individual partner entities and reported to the partners by a K-1 form. The information is then transferred to Schedule E on the partner's tax return. Partners are considered as self-employed and pay self-employment tax on their individual profits. The partnership files an IRS form 1065, which is normally filed by March 15 of the following year.

Joint Venture

A *joint venture* is a cooperative enterprise entered into by two or more business entities for the purpose of a specific project or other business activity. Tax consideration and reporting depend on the agreement between these entities regarding the joint venture's business structure—as a partnership or another entity such as a corporation, for example.

Limited Liability Company

An LLC may have one or more owners, called *members*. It is created through an operating agreement and is registered with the office of the Secretary of State in the state having jurisdiction over this business entity. The purpose of an LLC is to transfer legal liability from an individual—i.e. sole proprietorship or partnership—to the LLC entity; this action limits the liability to their investment in the business. Since the IRS does not have a filing category for LLCs, profits or losses are reported similarly to sole proprietorships or partnerships for tax purposes.

*C Corporation

Ownership of a corporation is by shareholders, and profits are distributed as dividends. A C Corp is subject to a corporate tax rate, and the corporation is a separate entity from the owners; therefore, liability from the business does not pass through to them. Additionally, those who work for the corporation are employees. Social security and other taxes are withheld by the corporation and paid to the appropriate government entity. Corporations are formed by registering with the Secretary of State's office in the appropriate jurisdiction. Additionally, the responsible party for the corporation is its board of directors. The functioning head of a corporation is the chief executive officer (CEO), who is responsible for the corporate activities. In most large corporations, another position of chief operating officer (COO) may exist. Other internal departments in large corporations are usually headed by vice presidents or directors.

Corporate entities file their federal corporate tax returns on IRS form 1120, which is due on March 15, or two and a half months after the close of their fiscal year. Corporations also may be required to file tax returns at the state and local levels.

*S Corporation

A special category of corporation is the S Corporation. Being a corporation makes it subject to the rules and regulations and the non-personal liability of the owners; however, there are limitations on the number of owners and only one class of stock. The S Corporation is not subject to the corporate tax table. Profits or losses are passed through to the owner/shareholders, who report these figures on an IRS form 1040 Schedule E. The S Corporation tax return is filed on form 1120-S. This is also due by March 15, or two and a half months after the close of the fiscal year. As is the case for partnerships, S Corporations transmit information regarding profits or losses from a subchapter S corporation's tax return to the shareholder through a K-1 form.

This notation is for organizations and operations where there is a direct filing requirement from the IRS.

Within the Business Organization

Businesses are legal entities and take the form of *sole proprietorships, partnerships, corporations,* or other entities as previously discussed. Additionally, there are areas of internal and external policies, procedures, and practices that must be managed and followed. All businesses must have proficiency in operational and administrative details. This means that to be successful, the company must perform to the satisfaction or expectations of its customers. Additionally, the company must meet external required reports and mandates. I have found the best way to manage the administrative and operational aspects of running a business is to identify the functions that need to be covered and assign a responsible party to them. It is recognized that smaller companies may not have the internal manpower to delegate the various oversight responsibilities to their employees, but other external entities may be hired to perform these functions. Please note that the company's management is still responsible to ensure that the functions are being addressed and that information is accurate.

One useful method of identifying these various functional entities and their connections is to make an organizational table, commonly called an *organization chart*. The organization table usually consists of boxes describing the function with lines connecting the boxes to indicate the reporting structures and also the connection between these and another associated function. What follows are brief descriptions of common areas found in most businesses. The organization should customize their org chart to their own relevant structures. Since businesses are unique, some functions are multilayered within a given department, and this area can be expanded or contracted per the needs of the individual business.

Primary Party

In a corporation, this position is normally the chief executive officer (CEO), who is also responsible to a board of directors. In a sole proprietorship, the position is usually called *president*. In a partnership, this person is called the *managing partner*. The responsibility of this position is to organize, direct, and control the functions of the company and to ensure that these other identified tasks/departments have adequate coverage and adhere to their responsibilities.

Accounting

This entity is primarily responsible for financial information such as revenues, expenses, purchases, asset valuation, taxes, and financial information supplied to relevant external agencies and organizations.

Legal

This department is responsible for complying with laws and regulations involving the company. This agent also assists in drafting agreements, contracts, and any lawsuits or disputes where potential liability exists.

Human Resources

This group is responsible for hiring; firing; lay-offs; training; employee benefits; labor law and regulation compliance; employee safety concerns; union issues, as applicable; compensation administration; and job descriptions.

Sales

The primary responsibility for this department is to generate revenue for the company through its operations and sales of its goods and services. Negotiations regarding pricing and the promises of services fall within this area. This entity is the customer's primary contact point.

Marketing

This entity is primarily responsible for letting customers know about the goods and/or services that the company offers. This is also the primary area responsible for advertising and other forms of communication, as well as initiating promotions to customers regarding the purchasing of the company's products or services.

Customer Service

After sales and meeting the provisions of the company's sales obligation, this area is responsible for making any alterations or insuring customer satisfaction with the company's goods and/or services.

Operations

This is the primary reason why the company is in business. It can involve manufacturing, retailing, services, or any combination of the three. Operations' primary function is to secure supplies and materials needed for fabrication or manufacture, or to provide the goods and/or services that generate revenue. Depending on the type of business, the operations function could be responsible for several other tasks such as logistics or getting workers to sites where the primary tasks of the company are performed. Since this is the primary functional aspect of the company, it is imperative that coordination with other entities in the business take precedent.

Special Circumstances

The above description of various functions/departments is not all-inclusive regarding the various situations involved in running a business. Unusual or unique circumstances will require some coordination of these functional areas and/or may be addressed by internal company personnel or external resources.

Chapter 2
Venues Used for Business

Once owners have determined their business structure and formation, they must next consider the business venue or what format(s) the business will use to operate. The following list consists of common approaches. Businesses are not limited to only one method, and it is common for a business to use various combinations to reach its customers.

- Brick and mortar
- Internet, social media, and catalogue sales
- Home-based businesses
- Pop-up venues
- Fairs and events
- Home and party plans
- Advertisements, word of mouth, and solicitation

Brick and Mortar

For most of history, people have conducted business at the physical location of the business enterprise, or at the location where the product or service is to be delivered. Although there are new approaches to a business's interactions with its customers, many people still desire a face-to-face approach. Additionally, a store or location affords the customer the opportunity to see, feel, and experience merchandise or receive information in person. Another advantage is that there is an expanded opportunity for explanations and other information about the merchandise or service. If inventory is kept at the business location, customers can inspect and receive immediate possession of goods. Another benefit of in-person interactions is the customer's ability to make a judgment based on the intangibles of human interactions.

In some instances, customer interactions take place at locations other than the enterprise's normal place of business; however, that meeting may prove to be challenging because of the nonavailability of tools, merchandise, or other items normally available at the business location.

Although there are some advantages to having a location-based business, some limitations also exist. Cost factors emerge such as rent, utilities, and scheduling staff for customer convenience. In many instances inventory may be limited in stock at the location, and the customer may still have to wait for the product to be shipped from a warehouse or a manufacturing facility.

Internet, Social Media, and Catalogue Sales

Due to the convenience of the internet, many businesses sell commodities via telephone or internet ordering. This practice is advantageous regarding the availability of merchandise. Since a larger variety may be available at a warehouse, businesses may have access to a larger inventory than at their retail location. Another facet involved in internet sales is the availability of merchandise owned by another company that is sold as if from your inventory (such as eBay).

Some problematic areas exist regarding internet sales. One is the sheer number of competitors selling similar products. For example, if a business owner wants to sell women's dresses, there can be over one thousand pages in a search program listing business that sell this product. Another consideration is the cost of shipping merchandise to customers, and in some instances its return. Many businesses offer free or reduced-rate shipping charges. This is possible because the cost of doing business via the internet is less than that at a location-based business.

Many companies are making a concerted effort to get merchandise to their customers as soon as possible, including several entities that have location-based businesses. In those cases, customers can order a product online and pick it up—including inspecting the merchandise—before gaining possession at these physical locations.

Even waiting for merchandise to be shipped to them or another physical location may prove to be unsatisfactory to customers if they are in a hurry to get the item. Another major concern for not-before-seen items shipped directly to customers is the return process if the customer is not satisfied with the product. Not only can this involve extra costs to the customer and/or business, but there is an additional effort expended by either the customer or the company's agent. Another negative situation can arise if the merchandise is either lost or stolen. Many shipping sources do not verify that the customer actually received the merchandise, and some dishonest persons may claim never having received the merchandise, or it may have actually been stolen.

Home-Based Businesses

The availability of the internet, computers, and other innovations have allowed many people to work jobs and run businesses from locations other than a structured office or other standard business location.

Some advantages are the cost of having and maintaining an outside location and commuting to those locations to do work. Because of the current prominence of many businesses not needing a full-time office facility, there are companies that will rent spaces on a part-time basis. Some of these companies can even provide business telephone answering services. In many service-related businesses, the business's representative will often visit the customer at the customer's location or where tasks can be performed.

Some other considerations that could be problematic for a home-based business are unwelcome distractions, like other people in the home, isolation from others working in the business, and zoning or other restrictions on the use of a home property for this particular business purpose.

Pop-Up Venues

A relatively new business venue is the pop-up outlet. This has become prominent recently due to the availability of spaces in malls and shopping plazas that have lost many tenants. The nature of this venue is only to be available for a limited amount of time and expend a minimum amount on props or other decorations. This is somewhat similar to venues at fairs and other short-duration activities; however, it tends to take place for a longer period of time and is usually for a retail market.

Fairs and Events

Many locations have events where businesses can present their merchandise and/or services. This can involve venues such as home and auto shows, and even charitable activities. Many businesses may make a direct sale at these venues or gather information for future contact with customers. In industry-specific conventions and gatherings, a business can make critical contacts with suppliers and other entities that would benefit their business.

Home and Party Plans

Some of the largest cosmetic companies have used this venue for years. The premise involves individuals hosting their friends and acquaintances at a party where merchandise from the business owner is presented to the audience. The host usually receives merchandise or some other gratuity for hosting the event. The business owner then either tries to book future events with the participants, and/or convert them to repeat customers.

Advertisements, Word of Mouth, and Solicitation

Many businesses use advertising (such as street signs), referrals, word of mouth, and other methods of solicitation for customers. Although all of the aforementioned venues use these activities, some business owners use this as an exclusive method to attract customers and gain their business. An example of this approach is the so-called hawking of their goods on street corners and in other public spaces. Even though many who use this method would fall into a category of "unauthorized" businesses, the format remains popular; even registered businesses use this type of activity.

Chapter 3
Forming or Starting a Business

N ow that you are ready to open your business, there are logistical and operational tasks you must perform. I have listed some of these activities below:

- Securing physical assets needed to operate the business

- Securing permits, appropriate paperwork, and documents

- Interviewing and hiring employees, contractors, and suppliers needed to operate the business

- Setting a target date to commence the operation

After determining what venue(s) to use to run this business, you will need to determine what physical assets and materials you will need for its daily operation. These items can range from office and operational equipment to inventory, uniforms, and other things needed. In the planning stage, setting one budget for start-up costs and

another budget for operating costs is mandatory.

There are various means of acquiring physical assets. Aside from purchasing a new item, former businesses that are no longer operating may have assets that would be available at a much lower price. Other methods of procuring equipment includes leasing or renting. There are even possibilities where someone's personal assets could be used for the business. The key factors are having available assets, which will assist the business development and daily functioning.

Securing permits, appropriate paperwork, and documents

Those in regulated professional positions—such as doctors, lawyers, cosmetologists, or any other professions that require state or other certifications—are aware that they must have their credentials in good standing to open their own businesses. Regulations, laws, and ordinances also require businesses to have proper licenses or permits before they are allowed to operate. Most business licenses are issued by the city or county having jurisdiction in the location where the business has its legal address. Although some agencies may require a business license for each location of an operation, many will honor a business license issued in another jurisdiction through a reciprocal arrangement. This is most often used in service-related businesses.

There may be other requirements, such as insurance or specific training, in order to receive the license or certifications. Before beginning an operation, the entrepreneur should contact his or her local licensing organization to determine what is necessary and proceed accordingly. If forming a corporation or LLC, you must file an application with the Secretary of State of the appropriate jurisdiction. The Secretary of State's office requires a business name and will conduct a name search. If forming a sole proprietorship or partnership, a name search is not usually conducted; however, the business needs a DBA—doing-business-as—name for its official business. Many people choose to use their own name on their businesses, and some even elect to use some title having a personal meaning.

I advise that a name reflect the type of business operation. This will be a great help for potential customers to understand the business operation.

The entrepreneur should contact the IRS to obtain a Federal Employer Identification Number (EIN). This number is necessary for reporting employee-related matters and is also required by financial institutions before opening a business account.

Identifying and Employing Entities Intrinsic to the Business Operation

In any operation, the need will arise to have other people or organizations perform tasks or duties necessary for the business to function. These tasks may be performed by external companies, contractors, or employees. The primary focus of the new business should be to determine what tasks have to be performed and by whom. For example, if the business is a retail brick-and-mortar operation where customers are expected to enter, then someone has to be available to work in the business.

Some controversy exists regarding the proper status of a person who works as a contractor. This individual usually receives an IRS form 1099-MISC, which indicates that this person is a self-employed contractor. Persons in this status do not have Social Security and Medicare taxes withheld or matched by the business entity. In my experience, a *statutory employee* will cost an employer approximately 15 percent more per hour of employment. Many businesses would rather identify this person as a contractor instead of as an employee. The IRS has rules and guidelines that indicate their stance regarding how to classify these individuals. If the IRS feels that the individual is misclassified, it can impose penalties and request payment of the taxes not previously paid.

There are special rules where family members or those having an ownership interest in a business can perform work and not fall under employee tax consideration.[2] I recommended that the entrepreneur either contact the IRS or a professional who has experience with this situation.

Setting a Target Date for the Commencement of the Operation

After all is said and done, there comes a time when the business will commence. If the previously indicated tasks have been done, as the saying goes, "The moment of truth has arrived." The importance of setting a date to start the enterprise is that it forces the entrepreneur to attend to tasks and other considerations to be operational by a specific deadline. There may be circumstances that will change the timeline; however, in consideration of the coordination of activities, it is important to try to start as previously planned.

---

2   For more information on these rules, please visit the National Center for Employee Ownership (NCEO) website: *https://www.nceo.org/articles/employee-ownership-very-small-businesses.*

Chapter 4
Entrepreneurial Characteristics & Skills

The entrepreneur always searches for change, responds to it, and exploits it as an opportunity.

- Peter Drucker

We should all feel confident in our intelligence. By the way, intelligence to me isn't just being book smart or having a college degree; it's trusting your gut instincts, being intuitive, thinking outside the box, and sometimes just realizing that things need to change and being smart enough to change it.

- Tabatha Coffey

Many new business starters initiate their activities based on what they perceive to be a good idea or other considerations. If a business is to prove successful, the entrepreneur/manager must develop or master the following traits:

- Management skills
- Operational proficiency
- Understanding of administrative functions
- Planning and organization of the business activities
- Understanding their market and/or what customers want from this business
- Social, cultural, religious, and other norms that may affect the business relationship with customers and others
- Personal appearance and other impressions that may affect the attitude of those they interact with in conducting various aspects of the business
  - Courage to make tough decisions
  - Wisdom to listen to counsel and know when to take action.

One of the primary activities I do in seminars I have conducted is go around the room and ask the participants to give a statement regarding their business concept(s). Most of the time, the participants will volunteer information about their current career or other background. Their backgrounds, in many cases, do not match what is needed to start or run the businesses they want to operate effectively. No one ever said that a person has to have a formal education in business administration to start or run a business; however, you should ultimately have an understanding of correct business practices, norms, and requirements to be successful. I encourage participants to take appropriate seminars, read relevant literature, and seek guidance from individuals and/or other entities who can help them learn those things that will help their business succeed. Consideration #7 of the "Business 7," found later in this book, gives more detailed information for the business support team, which includes those entities available to help the entrepreneur successfully operate his or her business.

Let us address some of the aforementioned factors:

Management Skills

Many new businesses start as a one-person operation. Eventually, if the business is to grow and/or become more complex, it will need other people to carry out tasks. The key trait necessary for these other people or entities to perform their functions in concert to what the management is desiring is communications. This communication is best achieved by the manager understanding the need for the task and stating clearly what the task needs to accomplish. Management needs to convey the task and the desired outcome clearly, even if this is a routine task. I always advise entrepreneurs to put policies, practices, and procedures in writing. If the recipient is a vendor or contractor, the requirements can be communicated in the form of a contract.

Besides communication, management is also responsible for ensuring that any person or entity performing assigned tasks has the skills, knowledge, and ability to perform. If management does not take care to keep positive interactions with employees and other entities, the business could suffer as a result of bad relationships.

Operational Proficiency

For a business to function well, there needs to be an efficient, workable method of performing the essential functions of the business. An initial method of doing the tasks of the business may prove to be unworkable or outdated. In other circumstances, the market may not as yet have caught up with the business, or a number of other factors may affect the operation. It is the entrepreneur/manager's responsibility to determine what factors are affecting the proficiency of the business and to take the necessary steps to make adjustments or other alterations in the operation to keep it viable.

Understanding Administrative Functions

A popular adage states, "Ignorance of the law is no excuse." Failing to have required licenses, permits, or other documents—and failing to adhere to federal, state, and local laws and ordinances pertaining to a business—can lead to penalties, operational disruption, or even criminal charges, if not properly addressed. I believe that many businesses fail because of administrative compliance failures. Entrepreneurs/managers are responsible for knowing the rules and following them. This is another area where the support team proves essential.

Planning and Organizing Business Activities

Unless the business is a franchise, the methodology of the business operation falls mainly to the entrepreneur/manager. Some franchises may allow some variation in the operation; however, the purpose of a franchise is to use the franchiser's program model to conduct business. If a business starts as new, and even in the case of a purchased business, the new management has discretion in what activities are to be performed, how they should be performed, as well as when and why they should be performed. Entrepreneurs are encouraged to spend time in business planning before starting their businesses. These business plans encompass both a formal presentation, which is usually presented to investors and/or lending sources, and an operating plan, which informs the details of the operation. As changes in the business occur, these plans should reflect those adjustments and other new considerations.

Understanding Their Market and/or What Customers Want from This Business

In many of my conversations with entrepreneurs, they have expressed positive feelings regarding what product or services they think a customer is willing to purchase. My next question is what research, experience, or other factors have led the entrepreneur to believe that to be true. Many have stated that they detected an interest in conversations with friends and other potential customers. Others have said that since they personally feel strongly about their product or service, there is a customer base or a demand for their businesses. One way to test a market is to survey actual customers who have purchased their offering to see if their assumptions are true, or if they need to make some alterations to the product or program. Some customers may not see a value in the product or service, or may not be interested in the offering. To have a viable business, you must have a customer who is willing to pay a price that covers the cost of the good or service, and sales must happen on a frequent enough basis to justify having the business.

Social, Cultural, Religious, and Other Norms That May Affect the Business Relationship with the Customer

Some people believe that almost everyone wants a particular product or service. For example, people throughout the world—regardless of their language, economic status, and social standing—desire cell phones. In other venues, such as foods, there are vast differences in the types of foods and dishes that people from various cultures desire. Different nations have unique cultural norms that affect dress, behavior, and even consumption patterns. Vast numbers of immigrants and descendants from all over the world come to the United States. Even within the general society, regional, geographic, economic, racial, and other cultural and demographic factors can determine whether the public will accept a business's goods or services. An entrepreneur should be sensitive to how the social and cultural factors may affect a particular customer demographic or what approaches would be necessary to have success with that group.

Personal appearance and other impressions that may affect the attitude of those that they interact with in doing various aspects of the business

In many consulting meetings and seminars that I have had held with would-be business starters, I have noted a plethora of items affecting their physical appearances. I understand that fashions change, and other cultural norms are more readily accepted. The fact is that we all have biases that may have derived from earlier norms—for example, women always wore dresses or skirts, and men always wore ties. People will perceive favorably or unfavorably a person's choice of clothing, grooming, language use, and other appearance factors.

In the eyes of some customers, vendors, and other entities, these stereotypes may lead to judgments about a person's knowledge, abilities, or resources. Many laws exist that make it illegal to discriminate against others based upon prejudices and stereotypes; however, human beings do make judgments. It is not always practical to change one's physical appearance, but entrepreneurs/managers should emphasize making the best impression on those you wish to influence.

Courage to Make Tough Decisions

As we go through life, we frequently have to make decisions that affect our current and future situations. The nature of running a business makes this a common occurrence. It is common in human nature to put off making decisions that may be unpleasant until a later time; however, this could lead to more severe unpleasant situations, such as lost business, higher costs, fines, and penalties. The entrepreneur must not only be aware of situations that call for some action, but also take the appropriate action when and where necessary.

Wisdom to Listen to Counsel and Know When to Take Action

No one knows everything, and we see our individual thoughts only from our point of view. This is one of the primary reasons to have a support team of advisers who can help identify situations and possible solutions. The wisdom comes not only in being able to identify various solutions that are offered, but also in deciding on the appropriate action to take when there are many options. Usually, wisdom grows from the entrepreneur's own knowledge, experiences, and willingness to accept the consequences of the action. As former president Harry S. Truman once said, "The buck stops here!"

Part II

The Business 7
Identifying Customers & Markets
Gathering & Evaluating Data

Chapter 5
The Business 7

A s a guide, these are seven areas that every entrepreneur should consider when planning a business.

Much of the following information has been presented in previous chapters of this book. I present these seven considerations, while somewhat of a recapitulation of the aforementioned ideas, in a format that gives a sequence to information that every entrepreneur should include in a business plan (items 1–4); other information about necessary written documents (item 5); additional information regarding possible sources of funding (item 6); and those professions or other entities that can help a business function (item 7).

After several years of reviewing what steps a person should take to consider or start a business, I have distilled seven areas of consideration. Entrepreneurs usually must write a business plan before starting or articulating their business vision. The information contained in these steps should be a guide to any plan, and the order in which I present them gives an overview of how a successful plan should be followed.

1) What is *my* business?

Often, when asked what business you want to start, the answer comes back as a general statement about the industry—a restaurant or IT application, for example. There are many variations of every type of business. What is needed is a clear vision at the starting point of this business. We can dream about what we would like the business to eventually become, but we need to focus on the starting point. The entrepreneur should articulate a specific plan—for example, a restaurant can be dine-in, fast food, or an ethnic variety. Often, there are related operations in any business, but if these other operations take time and effort away from the start-up phase and are not core to the primary operations, you should defer them until you establish the business's primary function.

2) Who is my competition (What comprises the industry)?

Contrary to popular belief, there really is not a lot that is new under the sun. Technology and other circumstances may change how people approach things, but the fundamental reasons why things are done usually remain the same. For example, we marvel at the communications and entertainment provided by today's commonly called "smart" cell phones; however, their purpose is communications and entertainment. Although older technology—such as the wired telephone, vinyl records, and eight-track tape players—is now mostly out of fashion, these forms served a similar purpose in their time. In fact, some people still use or seek that technology. Even with new processes or displays closer to the so-called "newest thing," these older items and approaches are still alternatives to what has just come out.

Most people view competition as some entity that is doing only the exact or very similar thing as they are. They feel that the competition is the enemy and they have to get their competitor's business, or the competition will take their business. Competitors do not have to be in the exact same business. For example, a grocery store that sells cooked chickens is a competitor to restaurants that have this product as their primary offering.

Any entity other than your business that will satisfy a customer's need with their services or product is a competitor. A major benefit of having a competitor is that this entity has probably helped initiate a demand for your product or service, and it has established customer expectations and pricing for these services.

3) What is unique about my business as opposed to the competition?

In viewing human nature, you will find—as I have—that people are basically creatures of habit; they would rather go with a known than an unknown entity. Unless there is no competing entity in the marketplace or the competitor's offering becomes unacceptable to customers, a new business will have to overcome these barriers. Obviously, a well-known franchise would have an advantage, since customers are familiar with their offerings. Being a new or unknown entity in this marketplace makes it incumbent on the new entity to come up with something desirable and not offered by the competition. The new business must do something to stand out or differentiate itself from its competitors.

One dangerous practice is to try to do what I and others call *submarining* the competition by offering a lower price. Unless the new entity has a lot of capital to do this, which could eventually drive the competition away, a lot of resources can be wasted. Often the competition has established a price point that will support their business and have already expended funds to establish their business. These businesses usually have an advantage in price and reputation. The new business may use loss leader pricing and introductory specials; however, this is a special price that will not normally be available. These special offerings give the new business an opportunity to prove their value in becoming the preferred business.

4) How proficient am I in operational and administrative knowledge?

A business can only thrive if it provides satisfaction to its customers. A business that provides unreliable services or goods will not prosper. The entrepreneur should have expertise in the daily operation, or have someone with this expertise in a key position. As previously stated, people who formulate a new business venture in familiar industries—or who have experience in specific aspects of the business that they are starting—have an advantage over those who do not know the market or do not have the necessary contacts. Also, as previously noted, running a successful business requires a vast amount of administrative work. Since most people do not have expertise in many fields where there are administrative requirements, I recommend planning to include support personnel to address the administrative issues.

5) Written plans

One constant about the human brain, I have found, is that ideas are continually flowing through our thought processes. We make a list before going to the grocery store. We take notes in school, so later we can review what has been said. Mankind invented writing to keep a record of information.

In many seminars that I have attended, the instructor emphasizes the need to formulate a business plan. Usually, the plan they advance emphasizes a mission statement, objectives, threats, and advantages. I prefer to use an approach that considers why and how the entrepreneur views and should use this plan.

(a) Formal business plan

The formal business plan exists primarily for the writer to organize his or her thoughts regarding a specific approach, depending on his or her unique business model; would-be competitors and information about the industry, including overview and trends; the unique way that the business will stand out from similar businesses; personal experiences or those of other key individuals on both the operation and administrative side of the business; cash flow projections; capital requirements for both start-up and continuing operation; and other pertinent matters.

Aside from being helpful to the entrepreneur, this information is useful and normally required by potential investors or loan sources. Please note that banks and other loan sources have internal documents they require business owners to submit.

(b) Operating plans

Normally, outside entities who review the formal business plan will not require information about the nuts and bolts of the operation; however, the entrepreneur needs to know how the operation will flow.

Additionally, employees or other individuals involved with the business need to know and understand their duties or requirements and the expected operating procedures. If a business is location based, the owners must communicate the hours of operation and the daily operating procedures to the affected entities, such as customers, vendors, and employees.

(c) Start-up and operating budget

This document should be part of the formal business plan; it should separate front-end costs—such as equipment, fees, deposits, and other costs associated with starting the business—from those expenses arising from the normal operation of the business. I suggest separating the cost of operating the business into fixed costs—costs such as rent, telephone, etc.—and variable costs, which are any costs that change with the volume of sales, service, or, production.

6) Where do I get the money—*capital*—to start the business?

Now that you know approximately how much funding you may need to start your business, the question arises, "How and where do I get the money?"

(a) Self-funding

Many people start businesses in the middle phase of life (middle age). During this stage, we have gained experience and have a better sense of what direction we wish to go. Another advantage at this point in life is that expenses such as buying a home—or the expenses associated with children—may have lessened. For those of us who are or have been prudent savers, we have also accumulated resources. Another situation may be that a person has been laid off or has retired from a current position. Sometimes a severance package is available which could help launch a business.

Sometimes we can leverage other assets, such as a second mortgage on a home. Many people in this stage of life have also accumulated a high credit rating and have a large credit line on their credit cards. Although I do not normally recommend taking this risk, sometimes this can be a good source for getting cash for a short-term reason.

(b) Friends and family

Many younger entrepreneurs are able to get loans or gifts from friends and relations. Some of those relations will opt to make the transaction a loan; others, a gift; and still others may wish to become investors.

(c) Partnerships and other business formations

One of the advantages of this type of arrangement is that others can contribute capital to the business venture. In these types of arrangements, the entrepreneur does not have full authority or control, but multiple entities may bring more success because of their contacts and experiences.

(d) Grants and crowdfunding

Grants, especially from sources seeking a tax write-off, are usually reserved for nonprofit businesses. Whereas some entities may wish to contribute to a for-profit business whose business or idea they support, the process of crowdfunding is available. Those who make these contributions are not considered as investors and have no economic stake in the business.

(e) Secured loans

These transactions involve some item of value being used as collateral for a loan. This item could be a house, car, stock securities, or other article that the loaner willingly accepts. The item may remain in the possession of the borrower put in an escrowed location, as determined by the entity making the loan.

(f) SBA-related loan

The Small Business Administration offers different types of assistance regarding business loans. The SBA does not make loans directly, but they guarantee a third-party lending organization a percentage of the loan as repayment if the recipient should default. A party can go to the SBA website or contact the agency to get information on procedures involved in getting various types of loans.

7) The support team

As previously stated, businesses rely on various external entities to function. Even if an entrepreneur had expertise in a wide variety of areas, there would never be enough time for one individual to keep up with all the necessary information and tasks that running a business requires. This section discusses different agents and their relevance to the business.

(a) Accountants

As previously stated, the Federal Internal Revenue Service is the agency within the US that sets the rules for how businesses should operate, and they receive an annual report that indicates the business's financial activity. As tax laws and regulations change, someone must have the knowledge to comply with the requirements.

Accounting is the profession that addresses these areas. Business owners should be aware that not all accountants have the same level of knowledge or proficiency. As in many other professions, competency varies. An *income tax preparer* may have sufficient knowledge to prepare a business-related tax return, but he or she also may not have the accounting proficiency to prepare accounting documents such as income statements and balance sheets.

The highest level of an accountant is the *certified public accountant* (CPA) designation. Although the CPA may not practice in all aspects of accounting, he or she has received a formal education and demonstrated proficiency on a standardize test recognized at the state level. Other accountant designations include *IRS enrolled agents* and those who have registered with the IRS who have a PTIN—*preparer tax identification number*. There are others who are not CPAs who, through experience and education, can use the title of *accountant*.

(b) Attorney

Businesses are legal entities in their structure and subject to litigation if they fail to perform per contract or to the expectation of operating in a legal and professional manner. Entrepreneurs are better served if their business structures are set up in a manner that gives the maximum legal protection and the minimum liability exposure. Litigation can come from several different directions. For example, a product sold or installed by the business may prove defective, or it could harm a customer or their property. In other instances, there can be a misunderstanding regarding what a business committed to do versus what a customer expected. An attorney should be the primary source of assistance in this instance.

(c) Insurance broker

Most people have personal insurance coverage on their health, life, homes, and cars. Insurance provides payment when some activity happens that requires monetary compensation to rectify or assuage the situation. Many assume that coverage in one area will extend to other similar situations. A good example of this assumption would be a person having coverage for damages caused by an accident on his or her personal vehicle being covered if the accident occurred while using the vehicle for business purposes. Many insurers will deny this claim if they do not have commercial coverage or if the policy has no commercial rider.

Liability for a business can come from several areas. *Worker compensation laws*, which differ by state, normally cover employee job-related injuries. Additionally, customers, contractors, or other entities can sue a business for harm to property caused by their business. Most location-based businesses also have to be concerned about harm to someone who is on their property. In recent years, there has been an increase in lawsuits charging that a business failed to provide sufficient security, and other inferences that the business did not fulfill its responsibility to the public. Various insurance coverages can provide some monetary relief against such claims.

An insurance broker can provide policies and information to address these areas. In many instances an independent broker may have multiple providers, which would offer more competitive pricing.

(d) Banker

Many people think of banks as a repository for personal and business funds. They also think of banks as a source of business and personal loans. Over the past several years, changes in banking laws at both the federal and state levels have made it easier for banking corporations to operate in a variety of locations with numerous branches. Another growing trend is for banking services to be handled remotely, either by internet, cell phone, or mail transactions. In fact, many banks have reduced personnel within this industry. One other change of note is the centralized decision-making at many of the larger banks. The entities making loan decisions may never personally communicate with an applicant, nor will an applicant know of the factors the decision-making entity uses to make this determination.

Since there are fewer opportunities to interact with another human being, people often miss the chance to ask questions and develop an in-depth understanding. I recommend that an entrepreneur who is seeking to set up business accounts or apply for a business loan do so in person. Often, a knowledgeable bank employee can resolve questions or give guidance on how to receive the best consideration from their institution.

Something to note is the effect of the *credit score*, also known as the *FICO score*, in securing a loan. Prior to the birth of the FICO score, a person's credit history was included on a document called a *credit report*. The vast majority of these reports are compiled by three companies in the US: Equifax, Experian, and TransUnion. Because these reports have such a major impact on people's finances, US Congress passed a law requiring that these organizations provide a free annual report.

Although credit history information has traditionally been available to financial entities, many lending officials appeared to be subjective in their decisions. Two statisticians, Bill Fair and Earl Isaac, made a correlation between which behaviors in a credit report made a person a good or bad risk. The FICO scoring system came into being in 1989. The score consists of three numbers and is divided into ranges. Information for scoring comes from the credit reports of these reporting agencies and determines creditworthiness.

Although the above information is used for personal credit, which is a consideration for individuals seeking business loans, a company named Dun and Bradstreet reports business creditworthiness. Having what is called an updated DUNS (Data Universal Numbering System) number is the first step in the SAM—System for Award Management—registration and certification process, which is required for all government contracts. This organization assigns legal business entities a unique number for business credit monitoring and tracking purposes. Many lending institutions also consider a DUNS credit report a factor in obtaining many business loans.

(e) Trade and industry associations

Almost all industries have an association that is a conglomerate of entities who come together for support, information, and lobbying to governmental entities on rules and regulations affecting that industry. Although a business's competitor may also be involved with this entity, the association works for the best interest of those within the group. This also can give competitors a forum to work together on projects and even some subcontracting opportunities. I also advise developing a list of contacts and specialists familiar with the unique situations within a given industry.

(f) Chambers of commerce

A chamber of commerce is an entity involving businesses from a variety of industries. They are nonprofit organizations that are funded by member dues, and their primary reason is to advocate for their business enterprises. Affiliated, independent chambers function at the national, state, and local levels. The primary focus of these various chambers is within their areas of involvement—for example nationally, regionally, or locally.

(g) Business-related organizations

Aside from the various entities indicated in this section, there are numerous other private and governmental organizations available to assist businesses in the various aspects of starting and growing their operations.

Chapter 6
Identifying Customers & Markets

A t this point, you should be ready to initiate activities to get your business started. The truth of the matter is that you do not have a business until you have a paying customer. To restate information I provided earlier, the purpose of a business is to provide a good and/or service to an entity willing and able to pay for it at a price sufficient to cover the cost of doing business, and to provide the business a profit for its effort. The first questions that any entrepreneur should ask are who the customers are, and how are they:

- Identified,

- Informed of the product or service,

- Convinced to purchase the product,

- Becoming repeat customers

- Assisting in recruiting other customers

Although many entrepreneurs make these considerations after the business has commenced operations, they should be aware of these factors in the planning and starting phases.

Identifying Customers

Any product or service that a customer would purchase should fill some need or desire that a customer has. If customers are currently doing business with a competitor, then the new business's approach should be identifying if and how the new enterprise's product or service would be more suitable for the customer. If the product/service of the new business is not well known or widely used, then the emphasis should be on identifying customers that would benefit from the new business's offerings. Such methods as conversations or interviews with potential customers, observation of interactions between customers and their current vendors, or even hiring a professional research company can help obtain information regarding potential clients.

Informing Customers of the Product or Service

Another question new businesses should address is how to let potential customers know about their offerings, how they work, and their benefits. If this is a competitive situation, then information needs to be made available to potential customers about the benefit of using your business's products or services versus their current provider. If the product is unknown or new to the marketplace, then your business should emphasize educating the target customers about how your offering will benefit them. Some common activities to help customers become familiar with these offerings include giving samples, doing demonstrations, presenting a portfolio of the product, or providing in-person or media-related presentations, testimonials or references from other customers.

Convincing Customers to Purchase the Product

Customers buy goods or services because of their own needs or desires. Considerations such as price, usefulness, suitability, and convenience affect their decisions. The new business should ascertain those factors that the customer is using to evaluate a purchase, and then provide as much information as required by the customer to answer their questions. The correct statement is not, "I sold," but, "The customer bought."

Repeat Customers

For the increased viability of a business, any product or service customers consume must have repeated sales. Primary factors that influence this behavior are customers' satisfaction with previous purchases and positive feelings toward the business entity. There are many incentives that businesses offer their customers to keep them connected to the business. These incentives can be reward points, discounts, or other perks for their continued patronage. An enterprise's customer service approach is a major factor in the public's willingness to repeat the business arrangement. In situations where the business interaction may be a one-time event, former customers can become positive influencers for other future customers.

Recruiting Other Customers

Comments and recommendations by customers having previously used the business's product or service can help recruit new clients. Some businesses actively give prizes or other incentives for referrals. In many cases, these previous customers will happily give a reference for the business if they were satisfied with their interactions. Surveys or other polling methods are tools that can assist in determining these customers' feelings about the business.

Chapter 7
Gathering & Evaluating Data

I f the entrepreneur is now ready to start a business enterprise, he or she should perform the following tasks:

- Evaluate the level of the business at start-up

- Test and evaluate the business premises

- Formulate and monitor the operating plan

Evaluating the Level of the Business at Start-Up

There are several considerations to determine what level of readiness and activities are in place at the start of a business.

The highest level of preparation requires addressing most operational, administrative, and monetary matters. Other items include making the customers aware of the business, anticipating that these customers will patronize the business when it starts, having sufficient financial reserves to cover unexpected situations, acquiring insurance and administrative licenses, training employees, and consulting with vendors and other involved personnel so that the business is ready to function.

A lower level of preparedness involves some of the same factors mentioned above, but with some aspects not fully in place. The non-conforming considerations, while significant, are not so critical that they would create a delay in starting the operation, and you can address them after the business opens.

The minimum level at which to consider starting the business is an evaluation to determine if the lack of the aforementioned components can be overcome while the business is operating and if the entrepreneur is willing to take the risk that they can become successful even though there are significant shortcomings at this starting point. Some issues could include having insufficient start-up funding, little or no reserve money for unexpected situations, the inability to meet monetary commitments previously made, unexpected problems or events, or a misevaluation of sales, administrative expenses, or customer commitments.

The last level of consideration may include deciding that the business has too many requirements that cannot be met. The decision may be that the proposed business is not worth the trouble and effort it would take to make it a profitable enterprise. The entrepreneur has the option of trying again later when the identified problems can be resolved, or abandoning this concept altogether.

Testing and Evaluating the Business Premises

Many factors can affect a business's success. The purchase of a currently operating business or franchise may require additional planning and other activities if the new business finds that changes in the customer base or new technologies require alterations from the previous operations. A new business with no previous history will not only have these same issues, but it also will bear the burden of being an unproven entity. One method to determine the viability of an idea or business approach involves scaling down the operation during the start-up period in order to evaluate what is working and determine if some approaches need to be tweaked or changed. This approach gives the entrepreneur an opportunity to preserve capital and minimize expenses. This also provides an opportunity to determine what parts of the operation are working or need revising. I especially recommend this approach for those without a lot of experience in their business, as it would minimize possible disruptions in the operation.

Formulating Operating Plans

As previously stated in the section under the Business 7, every entrepreneur has been told that one of the first things to do is to formulate a business plan. As previously stated, a formal business plan should include those items mentioned under numbers 1–4 of the Business 7 section: the nature of the business, the competitive environment, the experience and background of the principal personnel, and an evaluation of market forces that would affect this business. This type of plan exists primarily to inform the entrepreneur, possible investors, and lending entities about the intended business. Also intrinsic to the plan is financial information, which speculates on the expected revenues and expenses during some period after the business begins.

A written plan for the operation gives the entrepreneur the ability to determine and formulate the specific *standard operating procedures* (SOP) the business will follow. This also allows the entrepreneur to determine who will oversee or attend to various operational and administrative tasks that are necessary to run the business. As in life, changes are always a constant in the business environment. The operating plan in place when the business started may no longer be the suitable plan in future operations. The operating plan should reflect the current processes and procedures, and changes should be made to it as necessary.

Good starting points in the operating plan include the following:

- Making a schedule of operational activities
- Making an activity organizational chart
- Organizing an administrative file/record portfolio
- Listing and assigning employee/vendor duties
- Listing vendors and what/how they will provide wares
- Listing contact information and expectations for support team entities
- Making a schedule of operational activities
- Making an activity organizational chart
- Organizing an administrative file/record portfolio

Making a Schedule of Operational Activities

There should be a regular flow to the work activities of any business. Although it is not uncommon for issues to arise that may require immediate attention, the business should follow a daily routine. Depending on the type of business and requirements, having a routine makes it easier for management and others involved in the operation to establish a normal process for doing the work.

Making an Activity Organizational Chart

Every business has both operational and administrative tasks that fall under the purview of a designated individual or entity; an outside company also can cover this task. A diagram indicating the task and the responsible party helps to organize tasks visually.

Organizing an Administrative File/Record Portfolio

Management should keep documents pertaining to the business organization—such as incorporation or LLC certificates, government licenses and permits, and other similar documentation—in a secure but accessible location. You should keep other information, such as contracts and other agreements, in a secure and accessible location as well.

Although outside entities such as accountants and attorneys may have copies of documents pertaining to the business, management should also have a copy of these documents in their archived files.

Listing and Assigning Employee/Contractor Duties

In any business operation, those involved should know what their respective duties and tasks will be. Although these tasks can change as necessary, those involved should have the skills, ability, and knowledge to perform them. These entities should also know the business management's expectations.

Listing Vendors and What/How They Will Provide Wares or Services

Vendors are those entities that provide materials, products, or services to the business. I always recommend having more than one supplier in case of disruption from the primary vendor. Some businesses have an agreement with vendors regarding prices and other expectations. By listing the preferred vendors and their backup, those managing the operation will not only have a ready listing of these vendors, but also they can better coordinate activities between the business and the vendor.

Listing Contact Information and Expectations for Support Team Entities

Management and other involved entities within the company should have access to contact information for those supporting entities that interact with the business. As the relationship with these outside agents may change, listings of key contact persons and their involvement with the business should be current and accessible.

Chapter 8
Johnny Johnson Scenario

The following is used as an example of considerations in starting a business.

Johnny Johnson Starts His Business!

(Subject) The entrepreneur is Johnny Johnson.

(Experience) He has worked in the lighting fixture business for Ajax company for the past ten years. In his employment with Ajax, he has performed lighting installation and worked as an assistant manager in product ordering and inventory control.

(Motivation) Although fairly satisfied with his treatment as an employee, he feels that there are many new areas of business that Ajax management (who has a fairly conservative approach to business) won't go into.

(Identifying the opportunity) Johnny knows several independent electricians who have worked for his current employer in the installation of light fixtures. He feels that there are opportunities in selling a wider range of lighting fixtures from very cheap to antiques. He identified the following opportunities:

1) Customers who will buy and install fixtures themselves

2) Customers who will pay an outside party to do the installation

3) Owners of houses and apartments that are being renovated

4) Builders of new houses whose buyers can select their lighting fixtures

(Start-up capital) Johnny has saved about $10,000 that he is willing to use for his start-up. He knows a few people who may want to invest in his business, and he has good personal credit.

(Market research) After several conversations with potential customers, he decided that the initial core of his operation will be selling fixtures at retail. He also feels that he can produce additional revenue by contracting the installation with customers; for the more technical code sensitive installations, he can subcontract this work to an electrician. Johnny can also offer sales through his website.

(Logistical and competition research) Now that Johnny has determined where in the lighting fixture business he wants to start, he investigates and reviews what other companies in his market are doing. He looks at specialty operations and major big-box stores that sell lighting fixtures. This valuation assists him in determining their pricing and operations. By doing this analysis, he is better positioned to differentiate his offerings from these competitors.

Johnny now needs to decide if he will have a physical location or strictly use an online approach. Although a physical location would be more expensive, it would allow customers to see an actual product. Additionally, by having a direct interface with customers, he would be able to provide more information. This direct interaction would also psychologically give the customer more confidence in the business and could lead to future business with these customers as well as getting referrals.

(Operational planning) Since deciding to go with a physical location, the following items need to be addressed:

- What would be a good location where customers would want to come (being attractive and safe)?

- What size facility would be needed for both a show area, storage, and other logistics such as an administrate office?

- How many employees would be needed for the various tasks such as customer interface sales and other operational or administrative functions? Should he hire employees or contract out various aspects of these functions?

- What are the fixed costs of his location-based business, such as rent, utilities, insurance, fixtures, and other business assets?

- What are local governmental considerations and fees?

- Will the selected location provide other benefits, such as being near other businesses that have a design or home-improving motif?

After determining the answer to these location questions, Johnny determines his start-up cost. He will also need to know the business's projected revenue over a period of time. He contacts the Lighting Association to obtain any financial information that they may have regarding the volume and average price of sales in this industry. Johnny also contacts manufacturers and other suppliers to determine the wholesale prices for his products.

(Administrative processes) Johnny needs to decide what would be his best business structure. He knows that a sole proprietorship is the simplest business format, and he can limit his personal liability by adding an LLC agreement. He knows there are others who would like to invest in his business and he could set up a partnership structure; however, this could prove problematic if someone become disgruntled. He decides that a subchapter S corporation will give him personal liability protection, allow him to sell shares to possible investors (as long as these investors meet the IRS requirements), and have profits or losses passed through to him and the other shareholders, similar to a partnership.

(Support team involvements) Johnny meets with an attorney to draft his articles of incorporation and contacts the Secretary of State to start that process. Once he has received the incorporation charter from his state, he contacts the IRS for his EIN and registration as a sub-S corporation. He also meets with an accountant to determine his accounting system, and they decide who will be the responsible entities for keeping track of the financial transactions and records. He meets with an insurance broker to determine what type of liability coverage best fits his operation. Johnny additionally meets with his banker to set up the appropriate accounts and processes a loan which he will use as a line of credit. He also contacts his suppliers to receive a 30 day net pay arrangement. This extra time will allow for customers to pay for their purchases before the business has to pay the vendor. He drafts an operating plan, which is discussed with his employees and other entities who interface with his operation.

(The start) Johnny selects an opening date and is ready to get started. **GOOD LUCK!**

Part III

Other Information

Small Business-Related Organizations

Homilies & Thoughts

Glossary of Business Terminology

Listed Regulator Websites

Chapter 9
Small Business-Related Organizations & Groupings

US Small Business Administration (SBA)

The SBA was created by Congress in 1953 as an independent agency of the federal government. Its function, as articulated in its mission statement, is to aid, counsel, assist, and protect the interests of small businesses.[3]

The SBA fulfills its mission by offering loan guarantees and assisting with government contracts, financial counseling, and other forms of aid to small businesses that meet the following requirements:

- Are organized for profit

- Have a place of business within the United States

- Operate primarily within the US, make a significant contribution to the US economy through payment of taxes or use American products, materials, or labor

---

3   For more information on the Small Business Administration, visit the SBA website: https://www.sba.gov/.

- Are independently owned and operated

- Are a sole proprietorship, partnership, or corporation

- Are not dominant in that field on a national level

To categorize businesses, the SBA has established standards for every private sector industry in the US through the North American Industry Classification System (NAICS). These standards use the number of employees and/or average annual receipts to determine which businesses are considered small, and these standards are industry specific. Some SBA programs of note are as follows:

- Contributing to outside business resources, such as SCORE and SBDIC

- The Equal Opportunity Loan (EOL) program, whose purpose is to relax credit and collateral requirements for small businesses whose owners live below the poverty line and cannot attract adequate financial backing

- Disaster relief loans for small businesses where a designation of a National Disaster had been made

The SBA generally does not provide direct loans, but partners with outside lenders such as banks. These lenders can achieve a status of "preferred lender," which indicates they do not need SBA pre-approval to make loans.

SCORE (An SBA Resource Entity)

Founded in 1964 as a nonprofit entity and resource partner to the SBA, their mission is to provide counseling and mentorship from volunteers, many of whom have retired and shown proficiency in some business function such as banking, law, accounting, management, marketing, etc. SCORE chapters exist throughout the country. Additionally, this organization provides seminars on various business-related topics, including starting a business, writing a business plan, and accounting and legal information, for entrepreneurs. SCORE works with chambers of commerce and a variety of other organizations to further advance the goal of forming and improving small business entities.

The Small Business Development Investment Company

The Small Business Development Investment Company (SBDIC) was established to regulate and help provide funds to privately owned venture capital investment firms. America's SBDIC network is a partnership that includes the US Congress, the SBA, colleges and universities, state governments, and the private sector. The first SBDIC program was initiated by the SBA in 1975 as a pilot program at California State Polytechnic University in Pomona, California. Since that time many other states have formed SBDIC programs, which function mostly through local universities. Unlike SCORE volunteers, SBDC employees are paid professionals. They normally work with existing businesses and provide management and technical assistance.

Women's Initiatives

In many areas of the country, organizations have formed to address the underutilization and formation of women-owned businesses. Since women and racial minorities have historically had difficulties in terms of obtaining capital and being included in networks, which are major factors in business formations, these special initiative groups were formed to address these shortfalls.

Military Veteran Initiatives

Former military service personnel continue to transition from their service into civilian life. There has been a concentrated effort by the SBA and other government entities to assist them in this transition.

The SBA and these other entities have provided programs and waived fees for US Veterans to assist them in starting businesses. Unlike the VA Home Loan Program, there is at this time no specific funding for veterans to start a business.

Minority Advocacy Groups

The SBA works with many local ethnic and minority business development organizations to advance business activities and opportunities within their groups. You should contact your local SBA office to receive information about organizations within your market locations.

State and Local Government Entities

Many government entities have taken the initiative to form small business departments within their communities. They see such activity as growing their business community, adding tax revenue from business activity, and gaining more employment for their citizens. These government entities may work with the SBA or chambers of commerce, or they may set up their own programs.

The Start-Your-Own-Business Industry

There are a variety of entities that advertise setting up businesses for a fee. They include legal, accounting, real estate, and other related organizations. They also include business brokers, loan originators, and franchise sellers. This group of entities works for profit and is intimately involved in the process of business formation. Although the SBA and related organizations may provide information and programs, ultimately all businesses need a network of professionals and other entities to function properly.

Chapter 10
Common Industry Groupings

The industries listed below (often referred to as *business sectors*) are my groupings of types of businesses which have common purposes and similar rules and regulations. Although a greater variety of classifications can be made for entities within each classification, it was determined that due to the many types of business operations, it is neither practical nor desired to provide more than basic information about these categories.

- Agriculture & food supply
- Mining, extraction and energy
- Manufacturing
- International trade
- Wholesale, distribution, commodity transportation, and warehousing
- Retail and sales
- Marketing and information dissemination
- Services, professional practices, and guild trades

- Education and training
- Technology and electronic services
- Financial services
- Governmental services contracts
- People transportation
- Nonprofit organizations

Agriculture & Food Supply

Probably the oldest industry in human civilization is that of agriculture and food procurement. In a general context, this category includes the cultivation and harvesting of plant life for food and shelter. It also includes the raising of and hunting of animals for food. The ancient industry of fishing can also be thought of in this category. Restaurants and grocery stores are normally thought of as retail businesses; however, without the food component, they would not exist. There are many types of businesses which are involved in the production and distribution of food and other agricultural products at both the wholesale and retail levels.

Some of the agencies having major roles in this sector are the Department of Agriculture; the Department of the Interior; the Food and Drug Administration; and State and Local Health Departments.

Mining, Extraction, and Energy

Another ancient industry for humankind is mining. This industry involves extracting natural materials that are used for such purposes as building materials; rare elements such as gold, silver, and diamonds; chemical ingredients; and fossil fuels such as coal, oil, and natural gas. Although the generation and distribution of energy are not similar operations as mining or extraction, energy-related businesses are closely related to the products from this sector and therefore are being included in the group for convenience.

Due to the current emphasis by the media, governmental entities, and the public on the environment and climate changes, there are issues related to litigation and regulation involving this sector.

Some federal agencies having major impacts on these industries are the Interior Department, the Department of Energy, the Mine Safety & Health Administration, the Environmental Protection Agency, and the State Department (with regard to international treaties and operations), and judicial mandates.

Manufacturing

A company that creates, fabricates, or assembles a product is considered to be a manufacturer. There are special accounting rules that pertain to this business format. The manufactured products can be finished consumable items or parts that are components of other commodities. Because of the cost of equipment, specific labor skills, and raw or preformed materials used in processes, this area is usually considered to be capital intense.

A manufacturer does have varying levels of liability, ranging from the design to the safety of the product. There is an absolute liability attached to any item manufactured that proves to be unsafe, even if there was no willful neglect on the part of the manufacturer. The manufacturer normally supplies a warranty on the product which is in effect for a defined period of time.

Some agencies having an influence in this sector are the Department of Commerce, Department of Labor, Department of Transportation, and other state and local agencies and departments having related interests.

International Trade

In the modern world of multinational corporations and worldwide supply chains, many operations may have parts and commodities originating from different places throughout the world. International trade is an essential element in the economics and business growth of every nation. Rules and specific agreements involving international trade are made through treaties or other agreements between involved nations. Anyone seeking to build a business within this sector must be aware of these arrangements.

Another factor affecting international trade is the use of tariffs. This is a tax placed on items being imported to a country. The purpose of these tariffs is to raise the price of imported items so that competing domestic industries will not be placed at a price disadvantage from the imported commodities.

Some federal agencies having primary effects on this sector are the State Department, Homeland Security (which includes the Department of Customs and Border Protection and the US Coast Guard), and the Department of Commerce (International Trade Division).

Wholesale, Distribution, and Warehousing

Any product that is sold to an entity who is not the final user is considered as being at *wholesale*. If an entity is not the manufacturer or originator of the product (frequently referred to as *middlemen* or *jobbers*), they will sell the item to the retailer at a price greater than what they paid (call a *markup*) or charge a fee for the processing of goods handled. A close function of many wholesale operations is the consolidating of goods at central locations (*warehousing*). The wholesaler is responsible for the distribution of these inventories to retailers.

Currently, many shipping companies provide for warehousing and logistics, although they have no investment in or ownership of the goods they handle. There are other companies who have an owner interest in these goods, and their function is to sell the goods to an entity which will sell the product to the final customer or another entity along the supply chain. Usually, items which are sold at wholesale are exempt from local sales taxes and may have other exemptions. The wholesaler's liability is usually limited to knowingly selling a defective item or having caused the product to be substandard or damaged while in their care.

Some federal agencies which have a large influence in this sector are the Department of Commerce, Department of Labor, and Department of Transportation.

Retail, Sales, and Marketing

Conversely to wholesale, items sold to the final user are considered to be sold at *retail*. The retailer adds another layer of cost to a product, which is its profit. Since most marketing and advertising efforts are directed at the final consumer, that category is associated with this industry. The retailer is responsible for the selling and delivery of the product to the customer. Furthermore, most initial complaints about problems with a product are directed at the retailer. Recently, many manufacturers have started putting a written announcement in the packaging requesting that customers contact them if there are problems with the item purchased; however, most customers will approach the retailer for satisfaction. The retailer's primary liabilities are similar to the wholesaler's in regard to knowingly selling a prohibited or recalled item, causing damage to the item, or fraudulent advertising.

Some agencies having a major influence on the sector are the Federal Consumer Product Safety Commission, other departments where the retail product would be part of their industry, local government entities such as a state's Department of Revenue (Sales Taxes), and Code Enforcement.

Services, Professional Practices, and Guild Trades

Service businesses can encompass various professions and skills. They can include such professions as medicine, law, real estate, construction, and many other areas where the primary purpose is to provide skills and efforts in performing tasks. Many of those falling into this category are required to have unique training, licenses, and skills. This category also includes individuals who perform lower-skilled and manual tasks. It is evident that the vast majority of businesses fall into this category. Often those who would normally be defined as being in the service category may also become involved with many aspects of these other categories. Liability for service workers can come from various areas. This can include malpractice, failure to perform to a standard, or causing harm to other persons or property.

Some federal and state agencies involved with businesses in this sector include the US Department of Labor hour and wage division; the IRS for employee-related withholding taxes; the Social Security Administration; OSHA; various state certification boards; and other entities which regulate services offered to the public.

Technology, Electronic Services

One of the more prominent business sectors is anything involving invention or technology and their application. This category includes information technology (IT), areas of computer science, engineering and design, areas related to social media, internet transactions, publications, television, radio, telephone, and other fields related to scientific and technological aspects.

These newer technologies overlap with many of the previously discussed areas and are intertwined with them. In every seminar I have taught within the past decade, there have been individuals who have developed skills that related to some aspect within this category. It is considered as one of the major growth areas for formulating a business. Due to the pervasiveness of information available about individuals and institutions, there is liability associated with the protection of information. Additionally, this is a category where fraud and other security issues are of great concern since the potential damages can be very great and criminals can access their victims from anywhere in the world.

Some federal and local agencies involved in this sector are the Federal Office of Patents and Copyrights, the Federal Communications Commission (FCC), and state Public Service Commissions.

Financial Services

Although those in this category can also be classified as *service workers*, financial businesses are somewhat unique in that societies are held together due to financial considerations. This category includes such fields as accounting, banking, investing, insurance, and credit services. One of the primary requirements of any business is to have money or other assets (called *capital*) available to start and run the enterprise. The success or failure of a business is calculated by its financial wherewithal. The primary motivations in doing business are the financial consequences. Similarly to the other aforementioned categories, there is an overlap.

Since the use of money, credit, and the accumulation of other assets have such a profound effect on business and commerce, there have been notable activities in enacting laws, regulation, and oversight for companies within these industries. There are many independent agents (i.e., insurance, real estate, and loan companies) who run their own businesses within this category. Since monetary considerations are such a critical component within our society, liability can emerge from fraud, theft, neglect, and other areas.

Some federal and local agencies involved in this sector are the Federal Reserve Bank, US Treasury Department, Federal Deposit Insurance Corporation, Consumer Financial Protection Bureau (CFPB), and state banking and insurance commissions.

Government Services Contracts

Many services which are the responsibility of governmental entities are contracted to private businesses instead of being performed by the internal employees of that governmental entity. Since payments come from public funds, there is a responsibility to ensure that the selection process is done in an equitable and legal manner. Considerations of availability, experience, price, and reliability are some determining factors used by the selecting entity. To avoid the appearance of collusion, fraud, or other criminal behaviors by those government officials responsible for making the bid selection, there are regulations and protocols which should ensure that the vendor selection is done in a legitimate fashion. There have been laws, ordinances, and other regulations promulgated within the past several decades to ensure that discrimination or favoritism are not factors in selection.

To secure a government contract or make a bid, a business may need to post a bond. This is to ensure that the bid is serious, and if the entity fails to perform per the contract, funds will be available to bring in a replacement. There are other administrative requirements that businesses must meet to be included on a list of eligible candidates. For businesses interested in working in this area, contact should be made with the appropriate governmental entity to determine the requirements.

Some federal and local agencies involved with this area are the Small Business Administration (SBA) and various internal contract compliance departments that are part of the federal, state, or local governmental entity letting the bids.

Transportation

Many of the aforementioned industries also have a transportation component. Since the use of planes, trains, ships, trucks, and automobiles is such an intrinsic part of modern societies, it is worthy of being listed separately.

Some federal and state entities involved with this group are the US and state Departments of Transportation, which have responsibility for vehicles that travel on public roads; the Federal Aviation Administration as the primary authority for flight vehicles; the Railway Safety Administration for railroads; and Homeland Security, which houses the Transportation Safety Administration (TSA) and the US Coast Guard for maritime matters.

Many professions within the transportation category require licenses, certifications, and other authorization.

Nonprofits

Businesses which are formed for societal benefits [under IRS Codes 501(c)(3), 501(c)(4)] have unique corporate structure. The primary difference between a nonprofit corporation and a for-profit corporation is that nonprofits do not pay federal taxes, and the excess funds after expenses are not considered as profits. Funds received or raised by the nonprofit are not distributed to shareholders. These moneys are used for the organizational purpose of the nonprofit. An additional benefit for this type of business is that it can accept grants and other donations, which become tax deductible for the donor. Like other corporations, people who work for these entities are employees. Since this book is directed primarily at for-profit businesses, readers interested in nonprofit formation and operational requirements can contact various local entities which specialize in the formation and operation of these businesses.

The primary federal agency involved with nonprofit organizations is the Internal Revenue Service.

Chapter 11
Homilies & Other Thoughts

I have found that various quotes and statements can remind an entrepreneur of the different aspects of founding and running a business. Here are a few:

The 24/7 rule:

There are twenty-four hours in a day and seven days in a week, and you have to sleep sometime. A person can only do so much as an individual. To be successful in business, you have to enlist others or delegate tasks.

Preserve capital:

Do not spend or use your capital until it is necessary. Do not get permits or incur other costs until there is a need and the time is appropriate.

The customer is always right:

In any disagreement, the customer's point of view normally prevails, as the business wants to maintain the best relations with its customers; however, businesses must always consider fairness and appropriateness. Sometimes the answer to the customer is "no."

Price is the primary consideration in most transactions:

Some believe that customers will only buy from the entity that gives the lowest prices. The truth is that people buy what they value. Some new automobiles cost under $20,000, and others cost more than $100,000. Both will take a person from point A to point B. Buyers place a value on the car they purchase for reasons other than cost, such as status and special features.

Employees are only interested in their salary:

The statement is that employees only care about the business if they get paid for what they do. Psychologically, people want their efforts to be appreciated, and they also take pride in their contributions. Many will go above and beyond for the sake of the business.

There is no loyalty in business:

The statement is that customers, vendors, and employees do not care about your business and will go elsewhere if they can get a better deal. I have found that, depending on an individual's ethics and motivation, many people will support a business that they like and want to see prosper. In many cases, customers will pay a higher price or employees will do extra work to help a business succeed. The key is that the business must also show itself loyal to these other entities.

Government entities are corrupt:

The statement is that businesses need to pay the minimum amount of taxes. The infrastructure of society depends largely on government processes and services. Regulations assure fair and equitable dealings and a so-called level playing field for businesses and the general public. Taxes and fees are the means government entities use to hire employees and conduct tasks.

All is fair in love, war, and business:

The statement is that if a business does not look out for itself, it will lose to the competition. While it is true that the business's first consideration should be its own operation and welfare, many businesses prosper when their industry prospers. There are numerous instances in which competitors cooperate for the good of the industry.

A business's primary obligation is to maximize profits:

Some believe that making a profit is the only reason a business exists. Profit is the main motivation for business activity. A business needs a profit to continue its operations, and investors want a return on their investments; however, businesses are part of a community, and maximizing a profit at the expense of ethical behavior or harm to the general public will not service the continued existence of that business.

Fear the 3:00 AM meeting:

Some entrepreneurs complain that problems from their business keep them awake at night and they can't sleep. Many business owners wake up in the middle of the night because of some problem or other consideration and then cannot sleep comfortably. Often problems are solved or new ideas come from our subconscious mind about this time in the morning. The term "sleep on it" is derived from this phenomenon.

Chapter 12
Glossary of Business Terminology

The following terms are part of the business vocabulary, and aspiring entrepreneurs should be familiar with them.

Agency

An entity that is not the owner of a product or service but either represents or acts as a conduit for the transfer of the good or service from one party to another.

Angel investor

An investor entity that primarily invests in businesses that would normally be thought of as having a lesser chance of success.

Asset

A tangible item such as equipment or money that is available for the business's use.

Balance sheet

A primary financial statement that indicates the monetary value of the assets, liabilities, and owner's equity as of some defined point in time.

Business enterprise

An organization owned and controlled by an entity for the purpose of supplying a commodity or service in exchange for something of value.

Capital

Any item such as cash or equipment—that a business uses for its current or future operations.

Crowdfunding

Entities who give money for some activity or enterprise without expecting an ownership role or repayment. The primary motivation is the advancement of some activity of interest to the investor.

Depreciation

An asset's loss of value over time. The annual amount is an expense.

Entrepreneur

A person or persons who form a business enterprise.

Expenses

The money a business spends on its operations.

External support entities

These are organizations and companies that are not employees of the business but perform tasks or activities which are beneficial to the business. These companies may be delineated through contracts or other agreements. Additionally, many of these entities have a fiduciary responsibility imposed by a code of ethics, as required by their professions. Businesses are also supported by government entities, universities, suppliers, and nonprofit organizations.

Financial statements

These are reports that reflect the business's current worth; assets, monetary liability; income and expenses; and other vital information regarding the business. They can include other statements such as cash flow and asset depreciation.

Fixed expenses

These are business expenses that occur regardless of the volume of revenue generated by the business. This is also call *overhead.*

Gig workers

Persons who perform tasks for compensation on an irregular basis and who may be classified as statutory employees, casual workers, or persons doing tasks and not reporting received compensation.

Illegal work

Activity that is unlawful and/or unreported to avoid taxes or other requirements. This type of work can include criminal activity or working without the proper licenses or certification. Please note that some activities that are considered as criminal in one jurisdiction or time period can be decriminalized or have penalties reduced by changes in the law.

Income statement

A primary financial statement that indicates revenues, expenses, profit, or loss during a specified period of time.

Independent contractors

These are persons who are considered as self-employed and perform some tasks for the business as specified by contract or directive. They are not considered statutory employees. The IRS has outlined several considerations to distinguish these categories since a contract employee does not subject the employer to tax contributions, as would be the case for a statutory employee. Primary considerations regarding contract employees include control and participation. If the contracting company sets the time, location, scope of work, and methodology for the task, then it has control. Additionally, if the contracting business supplies materials and tools for tasks, then it has participated with the contractor in the work. At the end of the fiscal year, usually December 31, the contracting company provides the independent contractor with an IRS form 1099 MISC.

Please be advised that this area is of major concern to the IRS and is subject to both their audits and other litigation. I advise business owners to obtain legal and/or financial advice from someone who has expertise in properly categorizing employees/independent contractors.

In some circumstances, persons who do not work as direct employees of the business report to the business's managerial team and may even work in conjunction with the business's statutory employees. In other circumstances, a nonemployee or casual worker may perform a task for the business and work for a short or temporary duration for the business. Depending on the circumstances and interpretations, management may have to determine their status as employee or independent contractor.

Investor

Any entity that gives funding or other items of value to a business enterprise for a share of the ownership in that entity.

Lending organizations

An entity that makes funds or other capital available to the business with the expectation of repayment, usually with interest.

Loss

The amount of revenue left that is less than expenses.

Manufacturing organization

This type of operation fabricates a material or item that can be a finished product or a component part that is incorporated into another product. Their processes can involve mixing, altering, or assembling materials into some designated product.

Profit

The amount of revenue left that exceeds expenses.

Retail

A sale to an entity who is the end user of the product.

Revenue

Income received by a business for its products and/or services.

Statutory employee

A person who works under the direction and *control* of the business's management. Businesses normally identify managers and professional employees as exempt and hourly employees as nonexempt. The exemption derives from federal labor laws, and in most circumstances, exempt employees do not have to be paid for working overtime, whereas nonexempt employees do earn overtime compensation after working more than a prescribed number of days or more than a prescribed number of hours in one day. These prescribed hours can be subject to labor agreements or other modifications such as working four ten-hour days rather than five eight-hour days.

A variety of other labor laws exist at the federal, state, and local levels. Many laws have a minimum number of employee requirement thresholds, and assistance in determining coverage should involve a human resources professional or an attorney.

Government entities require that the employer collect appropriate taxes from the employee and pay them—along with other employee-related taxes—to that governmental entity. Employers also contribute an equal amount for the employee's Social Security and Medicare accounts. At the end of the employee's fiscal year—normally after December 31—employers provide an IRS form W-2, which summarizes the employee's earnings, taxes withheld, and other data for specific categories.

Variable expenses

These are expenses that change in amount depending on the volume of work and cost.

Wholesale

This designation represents a product sold to someone who is not the end user. Typically, the entity who purchases an item at wholesale will resell it to an end user for a higher price than they paid the product's originator.

Chapter 13
Listed Regulator Websites

A s indicated in other chapters of this book, there are various governmental entities that regulate or have a direct effect on different types of businesses and industries. The following is a listing of *some* of these entities, their description, and their URL listings:

Federal Entities

United States Department of Agriculture (USDA):

Involved with farming, fishing, and other agricultural programs.

www.usda.gov

United States Food and Drug Administration (FDA):

Responsible for food and drug safety.

www.fda.gov

United States Forest Service (USFS):

Responsible for forest management.

www.fs.fed.gov

United States Department of Interior (DOI):

Manages public land and minerals as well as several other areas.

www.doi.gov

United States Fish and Wildlife Service:

Part of the Department of the Interior; among other things, regulates commercial fishing.

www.fws.gov

US Department of Energy (DOE):

Responsible for administrating energy policy.

www.energy.gov

US Mine Safety Health Administration (MSHA):

Part of the Department of Labor; primarily responsible for promoting mine safety and health.

www.msha.gov

US Environmental Protection Agency (EPA):

Their primary mission is to set and enforce pollution standards.

www.epa.gov/

US Department of Commerce (DOC):

Their primary mission is to promote economic growth and trade.

www.trade.gov/cs

US Department of Transportation (DOT):

Their primary mission is planning and coordinating federal transportation projects and setting safety regulations for all major modes of transportation.

www.usa.gov/federal-agencies/u-s-department-of-transportation

US Department of Labor (DOL):

This department has multiple missions involving labor rules, employee safety (OSHA), and other matters pertaining to employment.

www.dol.gov/

US State Department of State (DOS):

Responsible for approval of any international treaty involving trade.

www.ustr.gov/federal-agencies/u-s-department-of-state

US Trade Representative (USTR):

As part of the executive branch, they work with the State Department in negotiating trade treaties.

www.ustr.gov//trade-agreements

US Customs Service (CBP):

As part of the Homeland Security Department, this agency is responsible for regulating commodities and materials allowed into the US from foreign countries and regulating import duties.

www.cbp.gov/

US Consumer Products Safety Commission (CPSC):

Responsible for the protection of the consumer from unreasonable risk and injury due to product safety concerns.

www.cpsc.gov

US Federal Trade Commission (FTC):

Primary mission is to prevent fraudulent, deceptive, and unfair business practices.

www.ftc.gov

US Internal Revenue Service (IRS):

They are responsible for setting rules for operating businesses within the US as well as administrating and enforcing US tax laws.

www.irs.gov

US Patents and Trademark Office (USPTO):

They are responsible for granting US patents and registering trademarks.

www.usa.gov/federal-agencies/u-s-patient-and-trademark-office

US Federal Communications Commission (FCC):

Responsible for regulating interstate and international communications by radio, television, wire, satellite, and cable systems.

www.fcc.gov

US Treasury Department, US Federal Reserve Board & US Federal Deposit Insurance Corporation (FDIC):

These federal organizations are involved with rules and regulations pertaining to banking and investment.

www.usa.gov/federal-agencies/u-s-department-of-the--treasury

www.federal-reserve.gov

www.fdic.gov

State and Local Entities:

Each state within the US has organizations which regulate, permit, or control various aspects of business within their jurisdiction. The following are some areas of responsibility at the state and local levels. Since their websites are specific to each location, the reader will have to research and locate those entities within their jurisdiction.

Insurance:

Most states have an office of insurance with an insurance commissioner as its head. These offices are responsible for the licensing of agents and enforcing regulation.

Banking and Finance:

Although interstate banking is now a reality, banks that are state chartered still fall under the administration and regulation of the state's banking authority.

Intrastate Transportation:

Any movement of commercial goods within a state's boundaries is under the purview of that state's Department of Transportation. Transportation of persons by public conveyance is under the state's authority.

Consumer Complaints and Fraud:

Although some of these complaints may fall under the jurisdiction of federal authorities, many may also violate local laws or may be addressed at the local level.

Licensing and Permits:

Most professional certifications and licenses are granted at the state level. There is usually some reciprocity agreement between states wherein an individual having been licensed in another state and having met other conditions will be allowed to gain a license or practice within this state.

Local Permits and Licenses:

Most local jurisdictions have processes wherein business that are registered or do business within their locations must receive permission from that jurisdiction by means of a license or permit. The fees for these documents may vary by business type, gross earnings, or other considerations determined by the local governmental authorities.

Thank you for choosing *The Busyness of Starting a Business: A Practical Guide to Starting a Business* as a foundational part of your journey in entrepreneurship.

Along with your continued research, industry education, dedication, and hard work, you can be confident that you are doing your due diligence in preparing for a successful business venture.

For more information on Busy Business Books or to inquire about booking Ronald Watkins for speaking engagements, please email busybusinessbooks@gmail.com.

Made in the USA
Middletown, DE
12 September 2022

10180364R10064